SCOTNOTES
Number 38

John Galt's
Annals of the Parish
and
The Provost

Ian McGhee

Association for Scottish Literary Studies 2018

Published by
Association for Scottish Literary Studies
Scottish Literature
7 University Gardens
University of Glasgow
Glasgow G12 8QH
www.asls.org.uk

ASLS is a registered charity no. SC006535

First published 2018

Text © Ian McGhee

All rights reserved. No part of this book may be reproduced, stored in a retrieval system, or transmitted in any form or means, electronic, mechanical, photocopying, recording or otherwise, without the prior permission of the Association for Scottish Literary Studies.

A CIP catalogue for this title
is available from the British Library

ISBN 978-1-906841-32-4

CONTENTS

	Page
Introduction	1
The Life	2
Enlightenment and Theoretical Histories	9
Annals of the Parish	12
The Provost	45
Conclusion	66
Further Reading	67

SCOTNOTES

Study guides to major Scottish writers and literary texts

Produced by the Education Committee
of the Association for Scottish Literary Studies

Series Editors
Lorna Borrowman Smith
Ronald Renton

Editorial Board
Ronald Renton
(Convener, Education Committee, ASLS)
Craig Aitchison
Diane Anderson
Gillin Anderson
Laurence Cavanagh
Professor John Corbett
Dr Emma Dymock
Dr Maureen Farrell
Dr Morna Fleming
Dr Simon Hall
Jean Hillhouse
John Hodgart
Bob Hume
Katrina Lucas
Ann MacKinnon
Professor Alan Riach
Dr Gillian Sargent
Dr Cheryl Simpson
Lorna Borrowman Smith

THE ASSOCIATION FOR SCOTTISH LITERARY STUDIES aims to promote the study, teaching and writing of Scottish literature, and to further the study of the languages of Scotland.

To these ends, the ASLS publishes works of Scottish literature; literary criticism and in-depth reviews of Scottish books in *Scottish Literary Review*; and scholarly studies of language in *Scottish Language*. It also publishes *New Writing Scotland*, an annual anthology of new poetry, drama and short fiction, in Scots, English and Gaelic. All these publications are available as a single 'package', in return for an annual subscription.

ASLS also produces a range of teaching materials covering Scottish language and literature for use in schools.

Enquiries should be sent to:

>   ASLS
>   Scottish Literature
>   7 University Gardens
>   University of Glasgow
>   Glasgow G12 8QH
>
>   Tel/fax +44 (0)141 330 5309
>   e-mail **office@asls.org.uk**
>   or visit our website at **www.asls.org.uk**

Note on the texts

The text used for these notes (and the page numbers attached to quotations from the novels) is contained in *Four Galt Novels* which also includes *The Ayrshire Legatees* and *The Entail*. They are edited and have an introduction by Ian Campbell and are published by Kennedy & Boyd, Edinburgh, 2015.

1. INTRODUCTION

John Galt (1779–1839) was a man of many parts, not all of which worked as well as he would have wanted. He was, at various times, a customs clerk, a businessman, a parliamentary lobbyist, a coloniser and, of course, an author. In the latter capacity he was extraordinarily prolific both in output and type. He wrote poems, plays, short stories, biographies, histories, textbooks, journalism of various kinds and, what he is chiefly remembered for, novels.

There are competing views about which of his considerable output of novels is his masterpiece. Claims have been made for *The Entail*, a family saga set in Lanarkshire, and for *Ringan Gilhaize,* a historical novel chronicling the religious disputes in Scotland from the Reformation to the Covenanters. But the novel which has unquestionably been the most popular in terms of editions, reprints and critical attention is *Annals of the Parish*. Close behind it in both popularity and critical attention is *The Provost*. Both novels are set in Ayrshire and, in their different ways, chronicle the changes which occurred during the sixty-year reign of George III from 1760 to 1820. They are full of acute observation, penetrating psychological insight, rich Scots language and, not least, great good humour.

2. THE LIFE

Galt was born in Irvine on 2 May 1779. His father was a ship's captain, engaged mainly in the West India trade. In 1789 Galt senior left the sea to become a ship owner and the family moved to Greenock. On leaving school at sixteen Galt began work as a clerk in the Custom House but left in the next year to join the merchants James Miller and Company where he remained until his departure for London in 1804. His time in Greenock was not all business. He was a voracious reader and avid theatre-goer, founded a Literary and Debating Society, went on walking tours to Loch Lomond, Edinburgh, the Borders and even as far south as Durham. He played the flute and joined a corps of volunteers, and he had begun to write poetry with verses appearing not only in the *Greenock Advertiser* but also in the *Scots Magazine*.

Despite this busy life in Greenock, Galt was worried by 'the narrowness of my prospects' and set off for London to seek his fortune in business. He had a slow start but in 1805 he joined with another Scot who was looking for a partner for his existing business. The company went bankrupt in 1808 – although like all good novelists, Galt did not waste the experience, and twenty-three years later incorporated it into his novel *Bogle Corbet* (1831). Later in 1808 Galt joined with his brother Tom in another venture, which also proved to be short-lived.

In 1804, after he had arrived in London, Galt had an epic poem *The Battle of Largs* published to less than complimentary reviews; fearing that being known as a poet would hinder his business ambitions, he suppressed any further distribution. Throughout his life Galt struggled to reconcile his commercial and literary selves. He could be very disdainful about authorship. In his *Literary Life* he states that 'I have ever held literature to be a secondary pursuit', and in his *Autobiography* claims that 'at no time, as I frankly confess, have I been a great admirer of mere literary character' and goes on to say that 'I have sometimes felt a little shame-faced in thinking myself so much an author [...] A mere literary man – an author by profession – stands but low in my opinion'.

Yet Galt could not stop himself from writing and had no small conceit of his worth as an author, which was just as well. The business success which he pursued as his preferred means of making his name and fortune proved elusive and he was repeatedly forced back to his pen to make a living. After the bankruptcy he researched material for a life of Cardinal Wolsey, the founder of Christ Church College, Oxford but the book remained unpublished for several years. Instead, in 1809, he decided to study for the law and entered Lincoln's Inn but, in poor health, gave it up after a few months. He went to the Continent to recover and spent the next two years travelling all the way round the Mediterranean, becoming friendly with Lord Byron and conceiving a scheme for British goods to beat the Napoleonic blockade of central Europe by taking them through Turkey. The scheme did not work.

He arrived back in Britain in October 1811 and by January 1812 he had published an account of his travels which was a modest success and paid for his journeys. The book on Cardinal Wolsey came out in June 1812 and also sold well but not well enough to keep Galt in the style to which he aspired. Moreover, in 1813 he married Elizabeth Tilloch, daughter of the owner of *The Star* magazine, to which Galt was a regular contributor, and he felt an even greater requirement to make a decent and reliable income. Business was still proving uncooperative so he subsisted by journalism on various subjects, and wrote for any magazine which would commission articles from him or accept those which he speculatively submitted.

By 1815, with one child and another expected, Galt was appointed secretary of the Royal Caledonian Asylum, a London-based charity for the children of Scottish soldiers and sailors, at a salary of £300 per annum. This was given up for yet another failed business venture but in 1819 Galt was appointed by the Union Canal Company to 'superintend' the passage of a Bill to enable completion of the link between Edinburgh and Glasgow. In effect he became what we would now call a lobbyist and used his London contacts to schmooze the Parliamentarians and neutralise any opposition.

This at least was successful and the grateful Company gave Galt a carriage, all expenses and handsome remuneration. At this time, too, his writing began to reach a wider public who received it with great acclaim. *The Ayrshire Legatees* was published in parts in *Blackwood's Magazine* from June 1820 to February 1821, and was then, in June 1821, issued as a book. In April 1821 *Annals of the Parish* was published. January 1822 saw the publication of *Sir Andrew Wylie* which has Galt, in the words of Ian Gordon, 'quietly initiating the political novel'. *The Provost* appeared in May of 1822 and *The Steam-Boat,* which had also been published in parts in *Blackwood's,* as a book in July. *The Entail* was published in December. If *Sir Andrew Wylie* 'initiated' the political novel then *The Provost* and subsequently *The Member* (1832) and *The Radical* (1832) consolidated Galt's claim to be the pioneer of that genre of fiction.

Books continued to pour from Galt's pen, with *Ringan Gilhaize* and *The Spaewife* in 1823, and all of this at a time when his business as a parliamentary agent was flourishing. In that capacity he had been approached in December 1820 by a group of Canadians who had played a major part in successfully repelling a US invasion of Canada during the War of 1812. They had suffered losses as a result and felt that the British government should compensate them for helping to retain a British presence in North America. They offered Galt a three per cent commission on any monies recovered, but explained that it would not be possible to advance any money for expenses. Galt was therefore committing himself to a great deal of work on a purely speculative basis.

Nevertheless, he threw himself into the task but quickly realised that while the government was full of sympathy for the Canadians it would not be paying them any money. The government did, however, hold huge tracts of lands which had not yet been surveyed or assigned to townships. Galt therefore hit upon the idea that a company could be formed to buy undeveloped land in Upper Canada from the government. In effect the company would buy land wholesale, divide it into smaller parcels, carry out some development in the way of roads and other infrastructure and then retail individual lots to settlers and emigrants. His expectation was that the price paid by the company would be used by the government to meet the claims of the 1812 war victims and to contribute to the expenses of the colonial administration.

It should be noted that at this period Canada was divided into Upper Canada (now known as Ontario), Lower Canada (now Quebec) and the Maritime Provinces such as Nova Scotia. The capital of Upper Canada at that time was known as York, but was later renamed Toronto. Each province had a Lieutenant-Governor, appointed by the Crown, and in Upper Canada the post was held by General Sir Peregrine Maitland, a man described by the Canadian historian Arthur Lower as 'crammed with the pet prejudices of religion, flag and caste'.

Galt's vision was that as infrastructure was provided and settlers began to prosper, land values would increase and the company would make considerable profits in the medium to long term. This is exactly what happened but unfortunately, largely because he failed to impress such a timeframe on the company, Galt's association with it did not survive long enough for him to share in the rewards his foresight had predicted.

Nevertheless, in 1824 Galt had managed to put together sufficient investors to form the Canada Company and began negotiations with the government to grant a charter to the company and to reach an agreed price for the sale of land to it. In June of that year the detailed plans for terms of sale were favourably received by the government. To reach an agreed valuation of the land, in 1825 the government sent a commission of five people, one of whom was Galt, to make an inspection and recommend a price per acre which the Company would pay to the government.

The final outcome was that the government agreed that the Company would purchase and be responsible for the settlement of 2,484,013 acres, purchased at 3s. 6d. per acre. Galt believed that the money paid by the Company to the government would be applied to settle the claims for the war losses but after the agreement had been reached he discovered that the proceeds were to be appropriated for the use of the Provincial government. He protested to the British government but there was no change of mind.

The Company was granted a charter on 19 August 1826 and Galt set off for Canada in October, landing at New York, USA on November 23. On the overland journey to York, Canada, Galt – as instructed by the Directors – studied the operations of two of the most respected land companies in the Genesee country of northern New York State and wrote back that his 'visits to the Pulteney and Holland land companies was most satisfactory'. Not only did the information he gained inform his views on land development and disposal but it provided the background and setting for the bulk of his novel *Lawrie Todd* (1830).

Galt got off on entirely the wrong foot with Sir Peregrine and with the Anglican, reactionary establishment of Upper Canada, who wrongly suspected him, partly because he was a Presbyterian, of being a radical. He also managed to alienate his Directors because profits were slower to arrive than they expected. All difficulties were compounded by poor communications, with letters taking at least eight weeks and more (usually ten) to get to London and return. It also has to be said that Galt's own personality was a major contributor to his downfall. He tended to behave as though whatever he believed to be right should be equally evident to everyone else. Consequently, he did not do enough to convince his Directors that this was a medium to long term investment and seldom tried to prepare the ground adequately for his policy proposals. When faced with opposition he resorted to affronted self-justification. Greater awareness of the consequences of his actions on other people and a much more diplomatic approach to the Provincial government would have buttressed Galt's position both locally and with the Company in London.

He was also hugely overworked, without adequate assistance and, although there was never any suggestion of misappropriation, his accounts were a mess and it was this that gave the Company, worried about the continuing expenditure without returns, the excuse to recall him to London in 1829 and to dismiss him.

Despite this catalogue of errors Galt was a very successful colonist. His investigations in the Genesee country provided him with a basic model and he refined it to fit the British and Canadian circumstances. He founded the cities of Guelph (the family name of the Hanoverian monarchs) and Goderich and the soundness of his method is borne out by the fact that it remained basically unchanged after his departure. The Canada Company went on to make considerable profit from the 1830s until it was finally wound up in 1953. On the morning of his departure in 1829 the settlers of Guelph presented him with an address of gratitude for his treatment of them and hoped that he would return.

Moreover, all three of his sons not only made their homes in Canada but built on his efforts to make a mark on the country. John became registrar of Huron County and Thomas was knighted as Chief Justice of Upper Canada. Alexander (1817–1893) was also knighted, having achieved both wealth as a businessman and acclaim as a statesman, being a principal architect of the Canadian Confederation and one of the first Canadian High Commissioners to Britain.

On Galt's return to Britain, and when news of his dismissal spread, he was sued for a debt he could not pay and was committed to the King's Bench prison for three months. To extricate himself he turned, as Sir Walter Scott did in his indebtedness, to his pen. Books and articles flowed from it, including two novels about his North American experiences (*Lawrie Todd* and *Bogle Corbet*), his autobiography, a biography of Lord Byron, a Scottish historical novel (*Southennan*) and two political novels touching on the debates around the Great Reform Act of 1832 (*The Member* and *The Radical*). He followed the first autobiography with another, *My Literary Life and Miscellanies*, which, apart from some reflections on his published works, was a collection of unpublished and reworked pieces of no great distinction. Nevertheless, he cleared his debts despite suffering a series of strokes from October 1832 onwards and having to dictate his work to his son.

In 1834 he came back to Greenock and lived quietly there, although still contributing articles and short stories to the magazines, until his death on 11 April 1839.

3. ENLIGHTENMENT AND THEORETICAL HISTORIES

Galt was a child of the Enlightenment, the name given to the intellectual and philosophical movement which swept across Europe during the course of the eighteenth century. It was characterised by an adherence to reason as the desired starting point for any enquiry and thus fostered opposition to absolute monarchy and to the dogmas of established religions. But it was not just about philosophical abstractions. It had a practical side with scientific and engineering advances in metal smelting, steam power, textile production and new agricultural methods which considerably increased the productivity of the land.

Scotland was particularly well-represented in Enlightenment thought with philosophers like David Hume and Adam Smith and engineers like James Watt. Galt read widely among the Enlightenment thinkers and absorbed many of their ideas including one which was central to many of his novels (including both the *Annals* and *The Provost*): that of 'theoretical history'.

The Enlightenment historian Dugald Stewart is credited with coining the term 'theoretical history', and used the method to postulate the likely causes of historical events and developments. Stewart stated that he would 'take the liberty of giving the title of *Theoretical or Conjectural History*' to the process of 'supplying the place of fact by conjecture [...] from the principles of their nature, and the circumstances of their external situation'. He went on to explain that

> when we cannot trace the process by which an event *has been* produced, it is often of importance to be able to show how it *may have been* produced by natural causes. [...] To this species of philosophical investigation, which has no appropriated

name in our language, I shall take the liberty of giving the title of *Theoretical or Conjectural History*.

This is exactly what Galt is doing in these novels with current developments in society. Actually, he did not see these books as novels at all. They do not have 'plots' in the conventional sense of the word and Galt admitted that his stories were 'greatly deficient' in that respect, but they do faithfully represent small communities which can stand as proxies for society as a whole. Just as scientific experiments may be made with a limited range of variables but the results then extrapolated to a wider application, so Galt's small communities can be used to illustrate universal truths and problems.

He said that his novels 'would be more properly characterised, in several instances, as theoretical histories' and that he has restrained 'the scope of inventions entirely to probabilities'. The same method applied today might be described as dramatised documentaries.

In the *Literary Life* Galt puts his case another way: 'Fables are often a better way of illustrating philosophical truths than abstract reasoning'. And philosophical truths were never far from Galt's thoughts. In the ferment of ideas arising from the Enlightenment one of the preoccupations of the philosophers was the discussion of society and man's place and functions in it. Galt was, however, a practical man and was less interested in abstractions or theories than the actual problems of man in society. It is these problems which Galt examines in the *Annals* and *The Provost*.

Kenneth McNeil provides a good summary of the 'theoretical history' approach when he says that

> Galt's output represents an effort to provide a broad overview of the economic forces that shape a society of a given space and over a given time. Galt rejected the category of romance altogether, which he felt was too devoted to the contrivances

and artifices of plot. Instead, historical "truth" is grounded in the logic of probability and exemplarity.

The *Annals* and *The Provost* can be considered as companion pieces. The former is ostensibly the autobiography of a parish minister and the latter of a merchant and local politician. In fact, the contrast is not between spiritual and temporal but reflects differences of personality and of location. There is considerable scope for comparing and contrasting how Galt deals in different ways with similar topics in each book but it may be more convenient in this volume to look separately at each text.

4. ANNALS OF THE PARISH

Introduction
The *Annals of the Parish* is set in a rural village and purports to be the autobiography of the Reverend Micah Balwhidder who becomes minister of the parish of Dalmailing in 1760 and retires in 1810. The precise location of Dalmailing is never specified, but it is clear from references in Chapter 2 that it is in Ayrshire; and Galt, in his *Literary Life*, says that it is modelled on the village of Dreghorn, although with elements drawn from the development of Inverkip, just over the border into Renfrewshire.

Dreghorn is less than three miles from Irvine, which is a Royal Burgh and is, of course, Galt's birthplace. It is also the setting for *The Provost*. The action of the novels is therefore confined to a very small geographical space, but that does not mean that the wider world is excluded. On the contrary, one of the purposes of Galt's art is to show how even these apparent backwaters are affected by the tides of economic, social and political change. That the setting of these books does not disqualify them from delivering lessons for other places and times is summed up by Frank Lyell when he calls them 'the perfect fusion of setting and character, and the universal truths of human nature through actions definitively localised in time and space'.

Galt, as has been noted, disclaimed the description of 'novel' for these works and preferred to call them theoretical histories. As Regina Hewitt explains, Galt wrote fiction, drama, and biography 'based on his observations of lived and recorded behaviour, elaborating on his "models" in ways he associated with the "theoretical" or "conjectural" methods of Scottish Enlightenment historiographers'. It was a consistent method, serving him well in the *Annals* and *The Provost* and was also applied to some of his later novels such as *Lawrie Todd* and *Bogle Corbet*.

Substantiating that the incidents in the *Annals* are drawn from life is Galt's disclosure in his autobiography that: 'when very young I wished to write a book that would be for Scotland what *The Vicar of Wakefield* was for England and began early to observe in what respects the minister of a parish differed from the general inhabitants of the country'.

Galt was fascinated by communities and in two later novels dealing with settlement and colonialism in North America, *Lawrie Todd* and *Bogle Corbet*, he examines how communities are formed; but in the texts under discussion he is much more concerned with changes to long-established societies and how these changes entail both winners and losers. Chapter 29 of the *Annals* describes the establishment of a new cotton mill which brings about an increase in land values and wages and thus 'a visible increase among us of worldly prosperity' (p. 67) but also 'signs of decay in the wonted simplicity of our country ways' (p. 66).

These swings and roundabouts are, as we shall see, a constant theme of the novels and they are shown as both good and bad because Galt is too accurate an observer to fall prey to either a blinkered nostalgia or an unthinking embrace of rising prosperity. It is this accuracy of observation, often based on real events, and clarity of vision which is the hallmark of both novels. It can also be read as a critique of the then-fashionable theory, current in the Enlightenment, and which it is useful to be aware of when reading these novels: stadialism.

Stadialism theorises that man developed through four economic stages, beginning as a hunter-gatherer, then becoming a pastoralist, leading to agriculturalist and finally reaching the summit of development as a commercial being. The theory gained wide acceptance and was used, among other things, to account for the assumed superiority of Europeans, especially the British, over indigenous peoples in the expanding Empire. They were still hunter-gatherers or farmers at best while Europeans had progressed far beyond these stages.

It was thus a justification for taking their land in order to cultivate the wilderness and to help bring the native peoples to a higher plane of civilisation; but the idea that the commercial stage represented a progression and that it was the summit did not go unchallenged, even at the time.

Adam Ferguson's *An Essay on the History of Civil Society* (1767) cast doubt on this view and suggested that much was lost as well as gained in achieving a commercial society. Duncan Forbes interprets Ferguson as saying that it is 'community that is likely to be a casualty in the progress of civilization' and that 'if you destroy community you destroy man's essential humanity and equilibrium and happiness'. This was a view which Galt tested by experience and observation. In the *Annals* and *The Provost*, Galt examined development and change in established communities over the previous sixty years, and it is clear that, while he welcomed progress, he did not see it as an unalloyed good.

Ferguson was also clear that the history of mankind was not about individuals. He said that human beings are to be taken in groups, as they have always subsisted. 'The history of the individual is but a detail [...] every experiment relative to this subject should be made with entire societies, not with single men.' This contrasts with the English philosopher Hobbes who viewed man as an isolated being with self-preservation and egotism as his guiding principle. Galt makes clear that he believes that community, rather than individuality, is both the driver and the necessary binding agent of society.

The Reverend Micah Balwhidder, whose autobiography the *Annals* is supposed to be, puts his own gloss on Ferguson with his exposition of the meaning of Christian charity, which is for the good of the community, in Chapter 35.

> I dealt with brotherly love, bringing it home to the business and bosoms of my hearers, that the Christianity of it was neither enlarged nor bettered by being baptized with the

Greek name of philanthropy [...] I told my people that I thought they had more sense than to secede from Christianity to become Utilitarians, for that it would be a confession of ignorance of the faith they deserted, seeing that it was the main duty inculcated by our religion to do all in morals and manners to which the new-fangled doctrine of utility pretended. (p. 75)

This is a key passage and has resonances with many of the themes which are addressed in the novel. It shows Balwhidder attempting to stem the flow of new ideas which was coursing through Scotland in the wake of the revolutions in America and France, the philosophies of the Enlightenment, the effects of industrialisation and the spread of commerce. They will be dealt with in more detail later in this Scotnote but at this point it is worth noting that Balwhidder clings stubbornly, almost desperately, to the old ways and appeals to his congregation to stick with what they know and not to be seduced by fancy titles or fashionable theories.

The novels can also be read in relation to another development in Scottish history, occurring twenty years before their publication. Sir John Sinclair of Ulbster, fired by Enlightenment ideas, wanted to measure as much as he could about the state of Scotland. To that end in 1790 he sent out a questionnaire to over nine hundred parish ministers, covering the whole of Scotland. This contained one hundred and sixty questions in four sections, namely:

- Geography and topography
- Population
- Agricultural and industrial production
- Miscellaneous questions

There were follow up questions in appendices – six new questions in 1790 and four more in 1791. The response was generally excellent, although some respondents needed more encouragement than others. The project was completed by

June 1799 and a full report was laid before the General Assembly of the Church of Scotland in that year. This is now known as the *First (Old) Statistical Account of Scotland*.

The aim was not simply, or even primarily, to record numbers but it was certainly meant to capture facts which would allow an estimate of the quantum of happiness enjoyed by the people of Scotland. Incidentally, the word 'statistic' is borrowed from German and originally meant 'of interest to the state'.

Galt was no stranger to the concept and had published a magazine article in 1807 entitled *A Statistical Account of Upper Canada,* based on information gleaned from his cousin William Gilkison, another Irvine native, who had explored that region. He also added a similar appendix to his novel *Bogle Corbet.* As might be imagined, the ministers in the real *Statistical Account* did not all stick to a straightforward answer to each question and the accounts for each parish vary enormously in how they are presented. Some vent the minister's own prejudices and parade their own pet hobby horses and it is this aspect of the process that leads Alison Lumsden to suggest that the *Annals* is, at least in part, a parody of Sir John Sinclair's great work.

Summary

The novel proceeds chronologically. Following the introduction each chapter is devoted to a year of Balwhidder's ministry up until his retirement in 1810 and each chapter is headed with the year and a summary of the events and topics which he will recount. It is therefore fairly straightforward for the reader to navigate a way through the book and to find specific events during the fifty years of Balwhidder's tenure. Despite this apparently straightforward construction the novel does employ the narrative device of *prolepsis*, that is to say it prefigures a future event. The introductory chapter tells us that his account will conclude in 1810 and throughout the text there are references to future events, such as mentioning a future wife when he is burying the first (p. 16), anticipating the decline in religious observance (p. 63) and in 1790 referring to an event which will take place some three years in the future.

This device is used not simply to alert the reader to forthcoming events but serves to subtly emphasise that the text is an autobiography. If an old man is looking back at fifty years of his life then incidents which he remembers will undoubtedly spark reminiscences of their sequels and it would be very difficult for him to confine his account to a strict chronological order of occurrence.

Structure
The introductory chapter references Balwhidder's beginning in Dalmailing and contains an extract from his final sermon on the occasion of his retirement. The chapter gives us an insight into his character and flags up traits which will become ever more apparent as his detailed accounts of the subsequent years will show. He makes much of the coincidence that he was installed in his charge on the same day as the accession of King George III to the extent that both were, in Balwhidder's view, 'preordained to fade and flourish in fellowship together' (p. 1). This equivalence of monarch with apparently humble parish minister bespeaks a proud inner conviction that he is marked out as a special case and an example of the Lord moving in mysterious ways.

The valedictory sermon is also revealing. He found his parishioners a 'docile and a tractable flock' (p. 1). Despite initial opposition to his placing they 'have lived to see the error of their way' (p. 1) which proves to his satisfaction that he was right and they were wrong from the beginning. Furthermore, they should certainly not agitate for political reform or attempt to rise above their stations since 'the best part of a Christian's duty in this world of much evil, is to thole and suffer with resignation' (p. 2).

Despite being a supposed autobiography, we are told virtually nothing about Balwhidder's early life. He says that he was brought up by his grandmother, as was his cousin who became his first wife, and that she was in Ayr where they were married (p. 6). We might therefore infer that they were orphans but no explanation is given. Nor is there any explanation as to why the patron has decided to offer the parish of Dalmailing to him. He simply arrives at the Kirk for his induction and the story begins.

Chapter 1 gives a much fuller account of that initial opposition to his presentation. Balwhidder was placed at Dalmailing by the patron and that action was met with strong opposition by the orthodox Presbyterians in the parish. The Presbyterian form of church government provides that congregations should appoint their parish ministers, while the Anglican church, at that time, provided that parish priests should be appointed by a patron, usually the chief local landowner. Sometimes patronage was not in the hands of one local landowner but vested in the Town Council, as happened in some burghs and was the case in Irvine and thus the Gudetown of Provost Pawkie.

The Act of Union in 1707 made clear that the Church of Scotland was the established religion of the state in Scotland and guaranteed its status but Scottish landowners complained that in losing the power of patronage they had lost a civil right. The argument found favour with an overwhelmingly Anglican Westminster parliament which also had suspicions about any measures which allowed the lower classes access to power, even at a village level. Thus, despite the terms of the Treaty of Union, patronage was imposed on the Kirk by the Patronage Act of 1712. Patronage became a running sore in Scottish affairs from the time of that Act, eventually causing the Disruption and formation of the Free Kirk in 1843, and disputes rumbled on until the practice was finally abolished in 1874.

John Galt's *Annals of the Parish* and *The Provost*

It is very difficult to overstate the importance of the Kirk to communities like Dreghorn at this time. It was the only form of worship that was openly available. Presbyterianism was, however, chronically subject to schism and in some places variants on Presbyterianism, such as the Secession and Relief Kirks, had been set up but these were not universal throughout Scotland.

More seriously, from Balwhidder's point of view and indeed of every orthodox person in Dalmailing, was the spectre of Catholicism. The establishment of the cotton mill attracts a few immigrants from Ireland and Balwhidder learns that a priest has come to say Mass for them. Galt uses this episode to demonstrate his own beliefs in tolerance, as he also does in political terms in *The Provost*. Balwhidder is all for having a stand-up fight with the priest but accepts the counsel of his elders that 'the days of religious persecution were past, and it was a comfort to see mankind cherishing any sense of religion at all, after the vehement infidelity that had been sent abroad by the French Republicans' (p. 94).

Nevertheless, and certainly at the start of his ministry, every soul in the parish was, at least nominally, a member of Balwhidder's congregation and thus subject to the Kirk's discipline. This was important because the Kirk was not just about religion but had civil and judicial functions as well. Rather like a Prime Minister and cabinet, the parish minister was supported by the Kirk Session which was made up of the elders, that is men (no women until well into the twentieth century) chosen for their probity or social position and who were appointed for life.

The Session had many duties including poor relief, appointment of the schoolmaster and supervision of the parish school, and a judicial function. Tom Devine states that:

> It exercised a close supervision on the moral behaviour of the parishioners and was the lowest court from which more

serious offences could be referred to the civil authorities. Indeed, the distinction between some ecclesiastical and civil crimes throughout the eighteenth century remained blurred. Kirk sessions heard cases of fornication, adultery, drunkenness and Sabbath profanation, but they often dealt with assault, theft and wife-beating.

The Church of Scotland holds an annual General Assembly of ministers and elders where matters both theological and political are debated. In the eighteenth century it was one of the very few bodies where a broad spectrum of Scottish society could have such discussions and could claim with some justice to represent the views of the people. There was therefore a strong incentive for the landed interest to maintain their power of patronage so that they could appoint ministers who shared their views and opinions. Since the government depended on the votes of the landowners they were reluctant to repeal the Patronage Act despite the widespread popular opposition to it throughout Scotland.

When the *Annals* was first published the title page was printed as:

Annals of the Parish
or the
Chronicle of Dalmailing
During the ministry of
The Rev. Micah Balwhidder
Written by himself
Arranged and edited
By the author of "The Ayrshire Legatees" etc.

At no point is Galt identified as the author of the work. Ian Gordon contends that Galt kept his public business and his literary activity in separate compartments and made a clear distinction between 'the "John Galt, Esq." who drafted memoranda for Ministers, and "the Author of *Annals of the Parish*"'. Nicholas Whistler, on the other hand, contends that both aspects of Galt's life were inextricably mixed and that to say otherwise is a 'damaging myth'. Neither man is wholly right. It suited Galt sometimes to present himself as a man of affairs for whom literature was a hobby. On such occasions, generally when he was writing about policy matters, he would play down his authorial celebrity by using pseudonyms. At other times he was quite prepared to trade on his own name if he felt that it would increase sales.

Whether stated explicitly or not, Galt was widely known to be the author of the work and, at this stage of his life, when he was surfing a wave of success in both business and literature, it suited him to keep separate personas. He seems to be enjoying the acclaim while coyly denying authorship. Presenting himself as an editor rather than an author also helps to put some distance between fact and fiction and is another aspect of his conception of 'theoretical histories'. It adds apparent verisimilitude, however contrived, to the idea that these works were indeed the product of real people rather than being brought forth from a writer's imagination. It worked, too, because just as today there are viewers who think that the characters in *Coronation Street* or *EastEnders* actually exist, so it was for Galt. His publisher, Blackwood, reported that his old mother became very angry at being deceived when told that the *Annals* was a novel. After the publication of *The Ayrshire Legatees,* which recounts the adventures of an Ayrshire family who go to London to collect a large legacy, Galt had to respond to letters addressed to his characters, and asking for money from them.

It is also worth pointing out that first person narration is Galt's favourite form. Most of his best novels and stories are written in that mode. It demands more of an author than the omniscient third person and can also demand more of the reader. If the sole narrator of the tale is the main participant in the action then how reliable or partial is his account? How far can the reader take the text at face value? Would the other characters necessarily share the narrator's perception of events? Galt asks us (and trusts us) to look behind what Balwhidder (and Pawkie in *The Provost*) are saying to make our own evaluations of their words and actions.

The Real among the Theoretical
Whether from a desire to increase the truthfulness of his work or from saving him the necessity of inventing episodes, Galt makes extensive use of real events. In the *Annals* he adapts things which happened elsewhere to the circumstances of Dalmailing. The scene in Chapter 1 where there is a disturbance in the placing of Mr Balwhidder and he has to enter the Kirk by a window was not unknown. There is no evidence that such an occurrence happened in Dreghorn but it did in various other parts of Scotland. T. M. Devine talks of 'the increasing incidence of bitter and violent opposition to unpopular ministers who were imposed on some parishes'.

Similarly, much is made of the activities of Mr Cayenne, who has made some money in a plantation in Virginia but returns to Scotland because he is loyal to the British Crown and therefore does not support the American Revolution and the subsequent independence of that country (p. 60). Later, he uses his money to invest in the establishment of a cotton mill. Not far from Dreghorn is the Ayrshire village of Mauchline. There, Claud Alexander, having made a fortune in India, returned and bought the estate of Ballochmyle where he built a Palladian mansion and then went on to build the Catrine cotton mill using the waters of the River Ayr to power it and, as a result, creating a whole new village. Incidentally, Burns delivered his poem 'The Bonny Lass o' Ballochmyle' with a letter to Claud's sister Wilhelmina. According to one of Claud's descendants, she was delighted while Claud was furious.

The real events of the wider world are also shown to impinge on Dalmailing. In 1776 a recruiting party, impelled by the need for troops for the American war, visits (p. 42). The French Revolution, on the other hand, is not mentioned at all in the 1790 Chapter. It is not worthy of note until the next year when it is described simply as what 'was going on in France' but then, proleptically, as 'the wild and wasteful hand which the French employed in their Revolution' (p. 69). Again, this is a realistic treatment because, earth-shattering as the Revolution was, it only impinged on a small Scottish village when the consequences had a direct impact.

The impact can be classed in two broad categories. The first was that the wars with France required soldiers and sailors, so some young men of the village enlisted which entailed consequences for their families. The second, and more far reaching, was that working people began to think about acquiring political and economic rights while the propertied classes worried about losing theirs and that, in turn, gave rise to great fear and repression.

The spread of democratic thought in the wake of the French Revolution and the repression of such views by the fearful middle and upper classes is highlighted in the trial of two young weavers (p. 73). The weavers admit to being reformers and claim that Christ was too. Mr Cayenne's response is 'What the Devil did He make of it [...] was He not crucified?' This is an adaptation of the remark attributed to Lord Braxfield, a judge of the Court of Session, in a much higher-profile trial of reformers. When the comparison with Christ was made he is said to have responded: 'Muckle he made o' that. He was hangit'.

As events moved on from the Revolution to the Napoleonic Wars the fear of invasion permeated Britain and, as in Dalmailing, there was a patriotic impulse to form corps of volunteers. Galt himself was involved in the formation of such a corps when he lived in Greenock, and while he salutes the patriotic motives he cannot resist the comic potential of the practical imperfections of such untrained would-be soldiers (p. 92).

There is also the curious case of the 10th Earl of Eglinton. In 1769 the Earl was walking on his land near the shore at Ardrossan when he came upon an exciseman, Mungo Campbell, who was carrying a gun. The Earl had strict rules about who could carry guns on his land because, as Galt has Balwhidder say, he was 'particular about his game' (p. 54). Apparently they had a quarrel about the matter and Campbell shot the Earl who died later that day of his wounds. Campbell was arrested but took his own life before he was brought to trial.

In the novel the incident is mentioned in Chapter 22 for the year 1781. Galt changes the exciseman's name to Mungo Argyle (although substituting Argyle for Campbell is not the most subtle of disguises) and allows Balwhidder a presentiment of his wickedness: 'I thought at times there was something no canny about him' (p. 54). He also rather thinly disguises the Earl by changing his title to Eglesham, as he does throughout the book, but otherwise sticks to the facts.

Gender

The Rev. Balwhidder marries three times but throughout his life he bears an unrequited love for the widow Mrs Malcolm and it is the subtlety with which this relationship is conveyed to the reader which demonstrates the extent of Galt's mastery in describing human nature.

Mrs Malcolm first appears in Chapter 1 and is described as 'a genty body' with 'pale hands' but always well-dressed 'as if she had just been ta'en out of a bandbox' (p. 4). She has five children and makes a meagre living by spinning linen (flax dressing was an industry in the Irvine area – Burns was apprenticed to the trade for a short time there). In the same chapter Balwhidder mentions his first marriage but it is a subject on which he has 'little to say' (p. 5). He has equally little to say when his wife dies in 1764, only that she was 'a worthy woman' (p. 13). He does, however, compose a poem for her headstone (p. 14).

This poem is one of the most artful passages in the book, not because it is good poetry but precisely because it is so bad. Galt has been able to replicate the kind of conventional ideas and forms which a country minister, of some education but little talent, would be expected to produce and with which he is inordinately pleased. So much so that he entertains the idea of going on to write a book although, predictably, the difficulty of such an enterprise means that it is perpetually postponed.

Balwhidder does not linger long as a widower. In the next year he marries again but it is hardly with wild abandoned passion. 'I had placed my affections, with due consideration, on Miss Lizy Kibbock' (p. 17). It transpires that his new wife 'had a geni for management' and is soon 'making siller like sclate stones' (p. 18). That page is also instructive in listing all the things which at that time might be done within a house rather than bought in from a merchant. Not that Balwhidder was at first best pleased with all the activity which he blames for preventing him from writing his book. He becomes reconciled when he sees how much money this industry makes and commends the second Mrs Balwhidder as 'the bee that made my honey' (p. 18).

When the second wife dies Balwhidder decides that he must soon marry again. The motivation is practical because he needs a housekeeper and in his coming old age 'a helpmate to tend me in my approaching infirmities' (p. 78). He rules out 'an overly young woman' or an elderly single woman since 'ladies of that sort being liable to possess strong-set particularities', so he looks for 'widows of a discreet age' (p. 78).

His first thought is Mrs Malcolm but he suspects that 'the saintly steadiness of her character' would lead to a refusal (p. 78). Instead he picks on Mrs Nugent, the widow of a professor, not least because she has no children 'to plea about the interest of my own two' (p. 79). The courtship consists of two visits and a dinner at which Balwhidder gives her 'a kindly nip on her sonsy arm' (p. 79) and they are married a year after the second Mrs Balwhidder's death with neither of them having had 'occasion to rue the bargain' (p. 79).

As a pious man, and a minister, Balwhidder never at any point says or does anything to disclose his feelings for Mrs Malcolm. She makes her appearance in Chapter 1 and from that point on Balwhidder exerts himself to help her and her family. He often 'happened to be daunrin' by' (p. 5) her house when anything of note occurs and his solicitude is obvious in every exchange – and there are many – with the family. His concern for Mrs Malcolm's family and his romantic side are shown when he defies Lady Macadam. She believes that Mrs Malcolm's daughter Kate is too low born to marry her son but Balwhidder thinks Kate is 'destined for a better station' and that 'surely their marriage is made in Heaven' (p. 38). He therefore performs the marriage ceremony and helps the young couple make a clandestine getaway.

There is a clear delineation between the male and female spheres of life. Outside the home respectable women may teach infants or instruct girls in necessary skills such as spinning and sewing or may keep a shop selling clothes or household articles which women would buy. Unless they are of a high class, like Lady Macadam, or of a very low one, like the 'light women' who follow the soldiers (p. 37), they are expected to know their place – which is to defer to men, at least in public. This condescension is shown even for Balwhidder's own daughter whom he describes as having 'a competent knowledge, for a woman, of geography and history' (p. 72).

Balwhidder, although himself morally unimpeachable, is not ignorant of the earthier aspects of male and female relationships. No minister of that time could be since the elders in the Kirk Session saw it as their duty to police the morals of the community. 'Antenuptial fornication' was a common crime for which the offenders would be tried before the Session and punished by being made to stand before the congregation for a number of Sundays. Two instances are highlighted for comic effect in the *Annals*. The gamekeeper Nichol Snipe seeks to mock the process by wearing two coats and two wigs, one of each back to front, so that he does not present his face to the congregation. Balwhidder exasperatedly tells him that if he had been 'a' back' then he would not have had to be there (p. 16).

The other instance (Chapter 13) shows also how class and education played a part in the Session's deliberations. A young man, licensed as a minister but not yet called to a parish, is charged with causing a pregnancy but since he is well-educated and employed by a local great family he attacks the Session rather than defending himself and threatens them with a defamation suit. This rather puts their gas at a peep and he is allowed to get away with it, although his subsequent behaviour shows that he was clearly guilty.

In both of these cases the women involved get short shrift. In the former she is anonymous and exists solely to provide a cause for Balwhidder to show his wit. In the latter she fares even worse since she and her child die before the birth. Galt had many progressive ideas but removing the double standard was not one of them.

Class
Society in these communities was a highly stratified pyramid. At the apex stood the Earl of Eglesham, a light disguise for the real Earl of Eglinton, and beneath him a layer of lesser landowners and, in the case of burghs, the more prosperous merchants and shipowners. In Scotland, the term for landowners was 'heritors', and the *Old Statistical Account* tells us that in the parish of Dreghorn in the 1790s there were twenty of them. These heritors had an important role since they were responsible for the maintenance of the parish kirk and manse, the stipend of its minister, the relief of the

poor, and for education. The practical effects and drawbacks of such a system of management are shown in Chapter 27 of the *Annals* when Balwhidder has to plead for repairs to the manse and then for an increase in his stipend.

Below the heritors were the respectable working classes, tradesmen, farm labourers, shopkeepers and servants. At the bottom were the feckless, the indigent and the physically and mentally impaired, all of whom depended, to a greater or lesser extent, on the charity of the parish or of individuals within it.

Galt was a lifelong Tory and believed in class divisions but his conservatism was overlaid by empirical observation and a basic fair-mindedness. He accepts that the weavers in the parish have a right to educate themselves and agitate for a more equal distribution of wealth. When a reforming bookseller opens a shop in the village, Balwhidder, who is otherwise a staunch defender of the Establishment, says that the man 'had very correct notions of right and justice, in a political sense'. He goes on, in what could be Galt's own credo, to say that 'conduct is a test that I have always found as good for a man's principles as professions' (p. 69).

There are also two passing references to race. Mrs Malcolm's son Charlie goes to sea in a merchant ship which sails to the West Indies with a cargo of 'live lumber' (p. 11). This is obviously a term for slaves. When Mr Cayenne comes to settle in the parish his household includes a 'blackamoor' servant named Samba (p. 60). Samba plays no further part in the novel but it is not to Galt's credit that his attitudes to race and slavery, as disclosed in his later novel *Bogle Corbet*, were ambivalent at best, although perfectly conventional for his time and class.

Technology

The Enlightenment of the late eighteenth century was a time of new thinking not only in philosophy but gave rise to new inventions in industry and new approaches to agriculture.

Balwhidder, in Chapter 29, describes how the Brawl burn was harnessed to provide power for a cotton mill and how Mr Cayenne, who had returned rich from America, was a major investor in the project.

There are many consequences. A new town, Cayenneville, is built for the people who come into the parish to work in the mill, and women are brought from Manchester to 'teach the lassie bairns in our old clachan tambouring [embroidery]' (p. 66). The result was 'a visible increase among us of worldly prosperity' (p. 67). Again, Galt points out that it was not an unmixed blessing. The old families resent the changes because 'it sank their pride into insignificance' (p. 66) and Balwhidder 'began to discover signs of decay in the wonted simplicity of our country ways' (p. 66).

The father of Balwhidder's second wife, Mr Kibbock, is a farmer who embraces new ideas because he 'had an insight of things, by which he was enabled to draw profit and advantage where others could only see risk and detriment' (p. 18). Galt provides as an example of the new thinking in farming the facts that Mr Kibbock plants trees on his land and brings new breeds of pigs to sell at the Glasgow market.

Community and Society
Galt was fascinated by communities: the way they grew and developed and the relationships and motivations within them. In his later life, researching for his role with the Canada Company, he paid particular attention to the growth of communities in the Genesee country of northern New York State and adapted what he found there when he came to create new settlements in Ontario. Within the constraints of time and circumstance that he had to contend with he was pretty successful, but his basic beliefs were shaped by his observations during his boyhood in Irvine and the surrounding parishes.

Galt was a product of the Enlightenment and had read widely among its prominent thinkers such as Adam Smith, John

Millar and Lord Kames. Their view was that humankind was on an upward path and that the commercial and industrial age led to the summit of human achievement. There were, however, dissenting voices like that of Adam Ferguson, whose view that community could be a casualty in the progress of civilisation was discussed earlier in these notes. Galt took a more nuanced view of this debate. He was not a Luddite. He recognised that industrialisation and increased commerce were inevitable, and that rising prosperity would float most − but not all − boats. As a businessman he welcomed such activity. But as a shrewd and keen observer he also saw that there were drawbacks and he points them out in these novels.

The increasing sophistication of the peasantry has already been noted as one of the consequences of industrialisation but it is not the only one. Balwhidder begins to see that the workers in these new enterprises included 'unsatisfied and ambitious spirits' who debated the ideals behind the French Revolution and had 'unsettled notions of religion' so that they did not attend Balwhidder's established kirk (p. 66).

That incident occurs in the year 1788 and, as for much of the eighteenth and early nineteenth centuries, this was a time of schism in Presbyterianism over what some might call minute points of doctrine. There were Burghers and anti-Burghers (those who would or would not take the Burgess oath), Lifters and anti-Lifters (when precisely the host should be raised during Communion), Auld Lichts and New Lichts (strict and somewhat less strict in accommodating to the new age). These differences produced new churches like the Secession and Relief Kirks, still firmly Presbyterian but, at least in their own eyes, of a purer sort.

Whatever the theological rights or wrongs, such disputes created fissures in what had been a remarkably homogenous society. Now, at the end of the eighteenth century, there were divisions of religion, incomers from Ireland, England and other parts of Scotland (especially Highlanders), new ways of working, including factories, and work opportunities for young women outside a home environment. There was more money and improvements in both private and public realms, but there were prices to pay. Galt records all this, but not in a didactic way. He is not preaching. He is pointing out how it would seem to a conservative minister who is unsettled by new ways.

Religion was not the only sphere in which dissension was becoming manifest. In the 1780s politics begins to be a cause of divisions in society. The ideas behind the French Revolution are taken up by the labouring classes and by some of the more progressive thinkers in the professional and landed classes. Weavers, of which there were many in Dalmailing, are at the forefront of agitation for democracy. Michael Lynch gives a number of instances of weavers leading strikes, protests and even an attempt to seize the Carron Ironworks.

At the beginning of the period, Balwhidder would have been astonished to find someone advocating universal adult male suffrage; but by the end of it, while still vehemently opposed by the Establishment, it was not such an outlandish idea. People who had known exactly their place in society were now rather less sure and either felt that they should rise or that they were threatened by such changes.

Global politics contributed to this uncertainty. The recruitment of troops to fight against the American rebels is recorded by Balwhidder (p. 42). All of these factors brought uncertainty and change to communities which had been stable for a very long time, and Galt is masterly in the way he describes the effects on society and the behaviour of the individuals within it.

As well as these weighty socio-economic issues Galt does not neglect changes to leisure activity since that is just as important to ordinary people. In 1761 Balwhidder inveighs mightily against tea drinking, although it is not clear whether that is because tea is smuggled or whether it provides an opportunity for women to get together. By the following year

Balwhidder admits tea to the manse, his opposition softened because it brings a benefit to Mrs Malcolm, and rationalised by allowing that it does not encourage drunkenness.

He also notes, with some wonder, that a bookseller has started business in the parish (p. 68) and that the weavers are subscribing to a newspaper (p. 66). Both of these developments suggest increased wealth among the populace and sufficient leisure to enjoy the extra money.

Language and Style
There is a persuasive argument that the most distinctive feature of the culture of the area in which the novels are set is the language spoken by the people. Galt himself commented, in the introduction to his short story *The Seamstress*, that it was a 'fortunate circumstance of the Scotch possessing the whole range of the English language, as well as their own, by which they enjoy an uncommonly rich vocabulary'. He also contends, in the same passage, that one result of this good fortune is that Scotland has produced 'among the lower classes, several poets, who, in the delicate use of phraseology, equal the most refined students of other countries'. He was thinking of the tenant farmer Robert Burns and perhaps also the Border shepherd James Hogg.

Galt wrote that at a time when even educated Scots like the philosopher David Hume and the biographer James Boswell were taking elocution lessons in order to speak in a more 'refined' manner, free of the supposed barbarisms of Scots. Galt has no cultural cringe about the Scots language. Instead he revels in it and plays it like an instrument from which he can produce a range of subtle tones and effects. In these two novels he moves freely through all the registers from broad west of Scotland dialect to Standard English and chooses specific registers for specific purposes.

The literary and publishing milieu in which Galt was working was conducive to deviations from the standard English forms.

Burns had shown that there was an audience for poetry in Scots, even outside Scotland, and Sir Walter Scott's novels which featured Scots dialect had been incredibly successful throughout the Anglophone world and beyond. The influential *Blackwood's Magazine* was published in Edinburgh and produced mainly by Scottish contributors. Scott tended to use Scots mainly for lower-class characters and for comic effect. Galt was much less condescending and used it for all the characters for whom it was the natural mode of speech and therefore it occurs in comedy, tragedy and the complete run of human emotions in between.

The strengths of *Annals* and *The Provost* lie not in plot but in character. Galt was a keen observer of people. He noted, and subsequently reproduced, their foibles and their vanities, their weaknesses and pretensions. But he not only looked; he listened very closely. The dialogue in these novels sounds completely natural, although it is often no such thing, but could only be made to sound so by an ability to remember the rhythms of ordinary conversation. That skill also enabled him to inhabit the minds of his characters so that he could reproduce how they would write as well as speak.

Annals of the Parish is written in a plain style. There is a minimum of Latinate words or high-flown rhetorical flourishes. In part this is dictated by the autobiographical format. Micah Balwhidder has had a university education but he is, and is very content to be, a simple country minister who does not seek to subdue his flock by the weight of his learning. When he writes the epitaph for his first wife he finds that Latin 'is naturally a crabbed language, and very difficult to write properly'. Besides, it would be inappropriate since Mrs Balwhidder 'did not understand the Latin tongue' (p. 14).

But it is not just the format. Galt tended to write straightforwardly and to avoid the ornate flourishes of some of his contemporaries. Nevertheless, language was a tricky area for him. He wanted his books to sell and that meant that they had to appeal to an English audience since England and English speakers in the colonies formed a hugely bigger market than Scotland. Yet he was trying to present truthful pictures of Ayrshire communities and that truth included the speech of their inhabitants. Emma Letley states that success for the Scottish novelist in the early nineteenth century depends 'on his writing with the Scots language without prejudicing the English market'.

Sir Walter Scott had paved the way. The publication of *Waverley* in 1814 had shown that the market would accept novels featuring the Scots tongue, although Scott is quite sparing in his use of dialect and tended to make sure that it related to characters that the reader could safely look down on. Galt was being altogether more linguistically ambitious. If these texts are to be taken as autobiographies then they must be written in the idioms of their subjects but they must also be intelligible to the target market.

In the event he trusted his readers to divine the meanings of unfamiliar words or expressions from their context. Credit must also go to his publisher, William Blackwood, who was in many ways a cannier and more cautious businessman than Galt. There is ample evidence of Blackwood demanding textual changes in later works, notably *The Last of the Lairds* (1826, but so heavily bowdlerised by Dr Moir at the instigation of Blackwood that it was not until 1976 that the text as written by Galt was published), but he sanctioned publication of these books in the form Galt wanted.

Nevertheless, this is not a literal transcription of the language of people who lived in Dreghorn and Irvine in the latter half of the eighteenth century: a verbatim account would have demanded too much of the reader. It is, however, a sufficiently accurate rendering of that language to be convincing and to be a vehicle for conveying its richness and resourcefulness.

Galt's Introduction and Chapter 1 of the *Annals* set the pattern for the remainder of the book in terms of both

John Galt's *Annals of the Parish* and *The Provost* 35

character and language. In the Introduction, as has already been noted, Balwhidder makes a great deal of the coincidence that his placing happens at the same time as the accession of George III – a remarkable claim for a country minister. He even sees a parallel between his retirement and the King's illness leading to the Regency. This is followed by the opening paragraph of Chapter 1 where we see more of his innocent vanity when he states that the three most important things to happen in Dalmailing in 1760 all relate to him. The order of occurrence is significant. First is his placing as the parish minister, but second is the arrival of Mrs Malcolm and last is his first marriage.

The Introduction is written almost entirely in Standard English but Chapter 1 is where Galt's language subtleties really begin to be displayed. Balwhidder notes 'my marriage *upon* my own cousin' (my italics) (p. 3). The paragraph contains no overtly Scots words but this is a Scots locution: in English it would be rendered as 'marriage to' and indeed in Ayrshire today it is still not unusual to hear of someone 'merrit oan tae' someone else. It is also seen in Balwhidder's use of 'mind' instead of 'remember'.

Scots words then begin to appear, with 'glar' [mud] and 'outstrapolous' [obstreperous] featuring in Balwhidder's account of his installation. When he directly quotes Thomas Thorl, a weaver, there are not only a number of Scots renditions of English words such as 'lang' and 'poopit' but examples of the Scots form of the past participle which has an 'it' ending rather than the 'ed' of English. Thus Thorl 'couldna have expectit' and 'was mindit' rather than 'expected' or 'minded'.

These patterns are maintained throughout the book. Balwhidder uses Scots forms and occasional Scots words. The working-class characters speak Scots in such a way as to convey the richness and distinctiveness of their language but not so broadly as to make their speech unintelligible to the English reader. More educated and refined characters like Mrs Malcolm follow Balwhidder's example, so that she 'canna take help from the poor's-box' but looks for 'the lend of that soom' (p. 5). There are three upper-class characters, Lord Eglesham, Lady Macadam, and her son, but only the latter two are given direct speech and they speak entirely without Scots. Thus are class distinctions signalled by modes of speech. The pattern is that for words which the characters would normally see written down, in Bible, books or newspapers, they will use English. For words which they would normally hear or speak they use Scots.

Graham Tulloch comments that 'Galt's work shows a careful working out of the social distribution of the Scottish language' but it also shows a differential use of language by individual characters according to the relative status of the character and interlocutor and the purposes of the conversation. He goes on to tell us that Scott 'was restricted by the association of Scots with speech rather than writing, with informality, the lower classes, the relatively uneducated and the older generation'. By and large Galt also observed these restrictions but, as Tulloch says, he found new ways of operating within them so that Scots could appear in reported as well as direct speech.

A first-person narrator in this locality will use English spelling and grammar, as an educated person would, but it is also natural that he will use significant amounts of Scots vocabulary. Tulloch sums it up by saying that 'breaking down the formality of the narrative opens up to the author a large potential for introducing more Scots'. And by putting the Scots language in the mouths of characters like Balwhidder, to whom the reader can feel superior, Galt makes it more acceptable not only to his non-Scottish readers but to those Scots, like Moir and Blackwood, who feared to be tarred with the brush of coarse provincialism.

Galt may have travelled far and mixed with the great and the good of Britain but he very obviously did not forget,

John Galt's *Annals of the Parish* and *The Provost* 37

and continued to revel in, the language of his youth to give him a literary scope which he would not otherwise have had.

Local Government
In a country parish such as Dalmailing there was no local government as we would understand the term. Education was the responsibility of the Kirk Session or of private enterprise. Poor relief was likewise administered by the Session (after a long and detailed examination of the applicant) and funded by the heritors who were also responsible for the minister's stipend and the upkeep of the kirk and manse. The Session consisted of the minister, who chaired it, and the elders, laymen who were recruited for their merit, piety or social standing and held the post for life. The clerk to the Session was often the local schoolmaster whose appointment to that post was one of the Session's chief functions.

As has been mentioned the Session also held quasi-judicial functions. As Tom Devine says, 'the distinction between some ecclesiastical and civil crimes throughout the eighteenth century remained blurred'. The minister was therefore a person with considerable power and was of central importance to the community. His attitude to morality, poverty, charity and community life generally would determine how that community operated. Galt chooses to make Balwhidder an essentially kindly man albeit one formed by fairly strict Presbyterian principles which he describes as 'the old and orthodox proven opinions of the Divinity Hall [at Glasgow University]' (p. 67).

Galt uses Balwhidder's old-fashioned notions to point up the changes which are coming to communities such as Dalmailing. The quote above is in the context of weavers who did not go to church but who were beginning to subscribe to the democratic ideas which had surfaced at the time of the American Revolution and which were to become much more potent as the events in France gathered momentum. Power is beginning to ebb away from the parish minister not only as a result of political ideas but also religious ones as new churches like the Relief and Secession become established. The monolith of the Kirk as arbiter of virtually everything within the village is showing cracks and the clues are all there in the *Annals*.

Balwhidder is not much concerned with personal advancement or pecuniary gain but these considerations are not entirely absent from his life. His monetary needs are taken care of by the industry of his second wife who was 'the bee that made my honey' (p. 18). He is originally disturbed by his wife's industry but he is very happy to take advantage of the increase in wealth to provide comforts for himself and to give his children a fine start in life. Nevertheless, he looks to the heritors for an increase in his stipend 'not because I needed it but in case, after me, some bare and hungry gorbie [minister] of the Lord should be sent upon the parish, in no such condition to plea with the heritors as I was' (p. 63).

It is clear, however, that he does not seek personal honour. His big opportunity in that respect comes when he preaches to the General Assembly and although he is complimented on his sermon he concludes that: 'Altogether, I found neither pleasure nor profit in what was thought so great an honour, but longed for the privacy of my own narrow pasture and little flock' (p. 52).

Irony

Irony runs through both books and is a principal source of their humour, especially the technique of ironic self-revelation. Kenneth Simpson says that it is 'a feature of Scottish literature' and that 'the *Annals of the Parish* and *The Provost* are masterpieces of self-revelation'. The Burns poem 'Holy Willie's Prayer' is a prime example of a man unwittingly condemning himself in his own words. In another context Adam Mars-Jones describes irony as 'like salt in cooking, something that can spoil a dish either by its absence or its indiscriminate use'. Galt's use is liberal but not indiscriminate.

There are countless (and disputed) definitions of irony but for the purposes of these books ironic self-revelation can be considered as the discrepancy between what is said and what is actually the case. The word derives from the Greek meaning 'to dissemble'. Balwhidder is generally dissembling to himself, as when he resists the offer of an assistant. Towards the end of his life the elders see that he is old and failing but Balwhidder contends that: 'I felt no falling off in my powers of preaching; on the contrary, I found myself growing better at it, as I was enabled to hold forth, in an easy manner, often a whole half-hour longer than I could do a dozen years before' (p. 102).

He is also dissembling about his true feelings when he pretends a disinterested concern for Mrs Malcolm and her children or when he feels threatened by the new thinking about religion and politics. The former case is driven by an unspoken and unadmitted love for the widow and the latter by the threat to ideas and opinions which he has always held. If they become questionable his whole world descends into turmoil. He therefore has to present his responses in terms which make sense to him but which the reader sees as no defence against the tides of history.

The interpretation of what is said is up to the reader. Some will take it at face value while others will ascribe varying degrees of truth, self-interest or self-deception to the words and actions of the characters.

There are also different qualities of irony, and Galt uses it for more than simple humour; although these instances are often funny, the primary function of irony in Galt's work is to underscore a serious point.

Society in Flux
Galt saw that change was consequential, cumulative and not wholly predictable. Opening a cotton mill or building a new road is a single act but how a society will react to the new circumstance cannot always be determined in advance.

In examining these communities Galt had the empathy of a native but, crucially, he had the detachment of one who lived at a distance. He also had knowledge about how the world actually worked, gained from his dealings with the business, political and literary elites of both Scotland and England. He was not a Luddite or an advocate for a return to some Arcadia which had never existed. He did not romanticise the society from which he came. He knew that the high-handed entitlement of a Lady Macadam, however amusing to read, would have been ill to thole in real life.

He was a businessman who welcomed progress but he knew that any advantages which it brought came with a price. He saw that there would be an increase in prosperity from the cotton mills, the new roads, the canals and the steamboats, but he knew that there would be casualties in more than one stratum of society. The weavers in the new factories and the lairds who saw their income and privileges reduced were both victims in this new world. As workers moved from land to factory there was an increased risk of alienation, and as bourgeois merchants gained wealth they sought to gain social and political influence, too, which in turn would bring changes to local and national government.

Two centuries later we can trace the influences which were affecting Scotland at that time but, as at any specific moment in history, there was no unanimity of view among those who were living through the changes which were occurring. The consensus among the foremost Enlightenment thinkers was that progress was an unalloyed good and that mankind, or at least the part of it that had the good fortune to live in Britain, was on a journey from darkness to light.

Galt's novels show, not quite a rejection of that view, but certainly a more critical interpretation of it. He sees and generally welcomes progress but takes the opportunity to remind his readers that there will be losses and that these losses are not trivial. Mr Cayenne and his ilk will bring investment and employment to the community but he will never have the feelings for the people that the traditional lairds, for all their faults, instinctively had.

The *Annals of the Parish* and *The Provost* are profoundly realistic. They may be theoretical histories but only in the sense that a painting is more theoretical than a photograph. The portrait of the culture is true, and if it had a soundtrack, the language spoken would also be true. The people portrayed are real and they engage in real events and with real issues in the societies in which they lived.

Balwhidder looks backward to a simpler time when the Kirk was the unchallenged ruler of the parish and certainties went unquestioned. He is highly uncomfortable with new modes of thought and behaviour. It all comes to a head in Chapter 29 when he debates with some weavers and is utterly confounded when they refute his arguments 'which were the old and orthodox proven opinions of the Divinity Hall' (p. 67). He clings to what he knew and believed when he was young and, despite the evidence of schisms in the Church and new political thought among the working classes, cannot bring himself to accommodate these new ideas into his worldview.

On his retirement Balwhidder is presented with a silver memento not by his own congregation but by the seceders, whom he describes as a 'Canaille meeting'. Canaille derives from the French for a rabble which is how he tended to think of those who deserted the established Kirk. Nevertheless, the gesture makes him wish for a time when all denominations of Christianity will come together and forsake differences of doctrine (p. 104). This is emblematic of Galt's own approach not only to religion but to life as a whole. He was always more prepared to judge by actions than by words or dogma.

Reception and Criticism
In the 1820s any novel by a Scottish author or on a Scottish theme stood in the long shadow cast by Sir Walter Scott.

His success, in England, Europe and beyond, was so great that comparisons were inevitable and likely to be odious. Contemporary reviewers seemed to feel obliged to measure any other author's novels against the master and most saw them as wanting.

On the publication of the *Annals* early in 1821 an exception was *Blackwood's Edinburgh Magazine*. This might have been expected since Blackwood was Galt's publisher, but there is a twist. The review, in the May 1821 edition, is prefaced by a note by the magazine's editor disclaiming partiality and saying that it is written by 'a distinguished writer who is a stranger to the magazine [and] is ignorant of the name of the author'. There is a strong possibility that the 'distinguished writer' is Henry Mackenzie, author of *The Man of Feeling*, a best-selling if somewhat lachrymose novel published in 1771 and which gave Mackenzie fame and influence.

The review states that 'there is no attempt at brilliancy of wit' but also that it is 'highly amusing to such readers as are fond of nature and simplicity' and commends 'the cordial communication between different ranks of the community which may preserve to rank or wealth its beneficial influence and to the lower orders the respect and attention which are due to superior station'. That comment seems to tell us a great deal more about the reviewer than the work reviewed.

The Inverness Courier must have pleased Galt by commenting that 'Micah Balwhidder is among our modern historians what David Wilkie is among the Scottish painters', since Galt corresponded with Wilkie and consciously modelled the *Annals* on Wilkie's genre paintings of Scottish rural life.

Other magazines were not so complimentary. *The Quarterly Review* seems baffled by the lack of a conventional hero and heroine and while 'it may please the reader for a few hours' it is 'not conceived with any great originality, told with any great force, nor contrasted with any degree of variety'. It is, however, scandalised by the remarks by Mr Cayenne, paraphrasing Lord Braxfield (p. 73), and avers that they are such as 'no gentleman could have uttered and no Christian Minister should have recorded'. It objects, too, to the allusion to the death of Lord Eglinton as 'not fit [...] for a work of this nature, [and] neither amusing nor instructive'. We can begin to see the prudery which would characterise the Victorian age and which would cause the falling out between Galt and Blackwood some years later. The latter had a better nose for public opinion and began to be fearful of being associated with what might be seen as 'coarseness' and 'vulgarity' in Galt's work. Galt of course was reflecting life as it was lived, rather than how the comfortable Edinburgh bourgeoisie wished it to be.

In June 1822 *The Edinburgh Magazine and Literary Miscellany* does a real hatchet job on Galt. The review begins by adverting to *Sir Andrew Wylie,* which had been published shortly before *The Provost*, and describes the title character as 'the snivelling, greasy, impudent, upsetting little porpus' and goes downhill from there. The author, 'whose epidermis [...] no critical shaft can penetrate', 'inflicts on us a transmogrified re-impersonation of the Reverend Micah Balwhidder'. It concludes that 'to write English is not *this* author's forte. The dog has, therefore, returned to his vomit again'.

The Edinburgh Review in October 1823 has a long article reviewing twelve novels by Scottish authors, seven of them by Galt, including the *Annals* and *The Provost*. They are described as 'imitations of the inimitable novels' of Sir Walter Scott and that Galt has sought to copy 'the humorous and less dignified parts of his original' although he shows 'a unity of didactic purpose'. Of course this entirely misses the point that Scott and Galt were trying to do two completely different things with their novels.

It should also be remembered that the magazines at this time were fiercely partisan in political terms and their reviews were coloured by the stance of the reviewer and what was perceived to be that of the publisher. They could also be, as in that from *The Edinburgh Review* quoted above, savagely condemnatory. It was this tendency which inspired Byron to write his satire *English Bards and Scotch Reviewers* (1809) to hit back at what he saw as unfair criticism.

The contemporary American novelist Ursula K. Le Guin compares Galt to Jane Austen and says that his humour 'though softer, is like hers – dry, subtle, morally loaded, and really funny' and that 'Galt *tells without showing*' (her italics). She goes on to say that 'small-town novels are intensely grounded; rich in satire, humor, and character, human affectations and affections. Intimate knowledge of one small community may yield psychological and anthropological insights of universal value'.

5. *THE PROVOST*

Summary
Like the *Annals*, *The Provost* provides the reader with a guide to the main events in the story by means of headings for each chapter. The chapters are arranged in chronological order but they are not given specific years, although actual dates can sometimes be inferred from the events which are being described.

Introduction
The *Annals* describes life in a rural parish but *The Provost* is set in a burgh and is the supposed autobiography of James Pawkie who, by dint of native cunning, rises from being an apprentice to becoming a prosperous merchant and the controlling influence in the town council. Galt had read and was fascinated by Machiavelli, the Italian author of *The Prince* (1513) whose name has become a byword for political cunning and deviousness. He had also had extensive experience of politics at the highest level in Britain through his work as a lobbyist, and *The Provost* is a distillation of that reading and experience by showing how a successful politician operates. It is set in a small Scottish burgh but although the stage is much smaller and less significant than Westminster the principles are exactly the same.

Like Balwhidder, Pawkie's story begins when he is an adult. All we know of his previous existence is that he served 'more than a year above my time' as an apprentice (p. 186). If the child is father of the man then Balwhidder and Pawkie are orphans. Where these two main protagonists differ, however, is that while Balwhidder is continually looking backward to a life, in his view, simpler and more secure, Pawkie is forward-looking and revels in change because he is always on the lookout for opportunities to enhance his income or his political power.

Drawing from Life

The location is rendered in the novel as 'Gudetown' but, as we shall see later, there can be no doubt that it is Irvine, a royal burgh with a town council (including magistrates) with responsibility for the administration of the town. The council then was, however, very different from the modern conception of local government.

There is a report by the Town Clerk of Irvine in 1710 in the burgh archives which is worth quoting at length since the situation was unchanged at the time Pawkie was writing:

> Their Council consists of fifteen merchants, including the provost, two bailies, Dean of Guild, and treasurer, and two trades, making in all seventeen. They elect their magistrates, viz., the provost and two bailies, yearly, the first Monday after Michaelmas; and the Friday preceding they leit [list] the magistrates and do put two on the leit to the old provost and four to the two old bailies, and the Friday preceding that they elect their new council, and on the Friday after the election of the magistrates they choose their dean of guild, treasurer, clerk, fiscal, officers, visitors of mercats, birlamen [low-ranking officers] etc. and are yearly obliged to change two merchants and two trades. And the provost and two bailies are not to continue above two years.

In this context 'election' means chosen and has nothing to do with a popular vote. The councils of the royal burghs were self-perpetuating. When a vacancy occurred the existing councillors chose the replacement and all the office-holders were chosen from within the council. Even the provisions about rotation and limitation of terms could be easily circumvented, as Pawkie repeatedly does. Such a system breeds endemic corruption. It is all too easy for a councillor, especially one as skilled as Pawkie, to rig estimates for work, to arrange favourable leases for himself or his friends and to dispense patronage.

Galt freely admitted that he had based the character of Provost James Pawkie on a real person, one Baillie Fullarton, who was a stalwart of the Irvine Council for many years and whom he had remembered from his youth. He assumed that Fullarton was safely dead but when Galt was granted the freedom of the Royal Burgh of Irvine in 1825 the ceremony was performed by the then nonagenarian Bailie Fullarton in a case of life not simply imitating but outstripping art. Galt commented that Fullarton's speech was worthy of Provost Pawkie himself.

The Provost is not specific about the starting date but it is clear from references in the text that it covers a very similar period to that of the *Annals*, until, in the last chapter, Pawkie states that he retired in 1816. It is also, supposedly, an autobiography, but it differs from the *Annals* in purporting to be a 'found' text. The introduction to the novel is written in the first person by an unnamed visitor to Provost Pawkie's widow. Galt soon introduces the ironical tone which permeates the remainder of the text by recounting that the widow adverts 'to the hand which, it is alleged, we have had in the editing of that most excellent work, entitled, *Annals of the Parish of Dalmailing*' (p. 185).

Describing the *Annals* as an 'excellent work' is both a sly joke and an encouragement to sales. There are other allusions to the earlier work in *The Provost* as when there is a reference to 'the stormy placing of Mr Balwhidder' (p. 199). These may be examples of metafiction but they also reinforce the realness of the accounts. It is to be expected that neighbouring communities would have a number of common relationships and people.

The *Annals* adopts and adapts events from elsewhere but in *The Provost* it is remarkable how true to place the local episodes are. Galt left Irvine in 1789 when he was ten years old so he must have had either an astonishing memory or a network of assiduous correspondents keeping him up to date with the happenings in the locality. There is, for example, a chapter on the successful application by the Earl for a lease of burgh ground (p. 211). In fact, the minutes of Irvine Council record that in 1804 the Earl of Eglinton applied for a lease 'longer than what is common' but the council agreed 'most cheerfully and unanimously' to restrict the lease to the normal twenty-one years because the inhabitants of the ground in question had 'an aversion to a longer tack'. The implication of the discussion is that the council expected the value of the area to rise and thus be able to let it again at a higher price.

In the novel the lease is granted to the Earl at a very advantageous rate through the agency of Bailie McLucre who, in return, gets a cadetship to India for one of his sons through the Earl's influence (p. 211). Galt has here shaped the facts to show yet another example of the corruption which was endemic in local government at that time. The councils of royal burghs were self-selecting so the only checks on the behaviour of the councillors were public opinion and their own consciences. Venality and corruption were therefore rife.

There are examples of this throughout *The Provost* and they are drawn from the life, although sometimes, as in the case of the Earl's lease, modified to fit a work of fiction. There is a description of how Pawkie speedily arranges for the council to pay for repairs to the kirk. These are carried out by a man who is also building a tenement on Pawkie's land and there is a clear implication that Pawkie has gained an advantageous private deal as a consequence of the work he promoted in the council for the kirk (p. 214).

The Minute Book of the real council shows that the need for repairs to the kirk was first mooted in 1768, but nothing happened until February 1772 when a plan for a new kirk was approved. The council received three estimates for the work and agreed on 16 March to accept the one from Bailie Muir who was, of course, one of their number. Galt incorporates the new kirk in the subsequent chapter to show that Bailie McLucre supported it for his own pecuniary gain (p. 213).

There are few occasions which Pawkie cannot turn to his own advantage. The prospect of a press gang coming to Gudetown seeking crews for the Napoleonic wars arouses his sympathy for the local sailors, but when the outcome results in public disorder and damage to his house he is able to secure compensation from the Government which not only pays for the repairs but also enables him to 'build up a vacant steading' which provides a dowry for his daughter (p. 224).

Not content with events, Galt also uses real people and the prime example of a real-life model is that for Provost Pawkie himself who, as mentioned earlier, was based on Bailie Fullarton of Irvine. Ian Gordon quotes many more examples of real events in Irvine reappearing in *The Provost* in his explanatory notes for the edition he prepared for the *World's Classics* series, including problems with a drunken town drummer and the several elections of the Earl of Eglinton, the chief local landowner, as Provost. During the Earl's tenure Pawkie is used as a kind of regent and that, of course, suits him very well indeed. It assists him 'to rule without being felt which is the great mystery of policy' (p. 189). He adds a gloss to this maxim by saying that it is 'a better thing, in the world, to have power and influence, than to show the possession of either' (p. 205).

The proposal to build an academy in Irvine is another interesting demonstration of how Galt's art coincided with and differed from the actuality. This issue is first mentioned in the actual minutes in 1813 when the council agreed to subscribe £300 for the school and to increase the salary bill by £30 per annum. The foundation stone was laid in 1814 and in 1815 the council borrowed £700 to complete the project. This was obviously not sufficient because in 1816 the council responded positively, although in a sum not specified, to a further petition to 'finish the Academy'. The *Ayr Advertiser* finally reports on the opening ceremony on July 11 1816 including the words 'we understand that the Magistrates and Town Council have since voted, from the Town's funds, a salary for a Rector and other sums towards completing this establishment'.

Galt puts the academy proposal as arising in 1809 and describes how Pawkie thwarted the plans (although Pawkie regrets that in so doing he loses the opportunity to have a wall on his property built at no cost to himself (p. 255)). The key part of this episode is Pawkie's comment that 'I do not think it any shame to a public man to serve his own interests by those of the community, when he can righteously do so' (p. 254). It is this ability to align private and public interest which characterises Pawkie throughout his career and which Galt, without being overtly censorious, clearly sees as becoming unsustainable.

Galt's satire is not savagely Swiftian. It is gentler and aims to nudge the reader rather than bludgeon her or him. He foresees that reform is coming and shows this in Pawkie's third term as Provost. Pawkie admits that he 'had a sort of sinister respect for my own interests' but on taking office 'became, as it were, a new man on the spot' (p. 259). He manifests this change by curtailing the council's expenditure on the traditional Michaelmas dinners (p. 261).

The model for this episode is the resolution of the council in 1820 to discontinue public entertainments on the king's birthday, although they did agree to meet in Milne's Inn 'as a social club' with 'such of the respectable inhabitants as are agreeable to join the party and drink His Majesty's health'.

Chapter 23 of *The Provost* is the key summary of how business was managed and how it can no longer go on in that way. As Keith Costain points out, Galt uses the death of Bailie McLucre to let Pawkie reflect on how change is inevitably coming to the burgh. Pawkie says that 'it seemed to be the use and wont of men in public trusts, to indemnify themselves in a left-handed way for the time and trouble they bestowed in the same' (p. 225). He considers that McLucre was 'the last remnant of the old practice of managing the concerns of the town' (p. 225) and that he had 'outlived the times for which he was qualified' (p. 226). Pawkie, on the other hand, has felt the way the wind was blowing. He can justify his former actions as well as his new policy because he has 'endeavoured, in a manner, to be governed by the spirit of the times in which the transaction happened' (p. 226).

Pawkie has played this system for all that it is worth but he perceives that a wind of change is beginning to blow. He tells us that the corruption was no secret and that it caused 'merriment and jocularity' among his neighbours (p. 226). He defends this as being part of the spirit of the time but he also sees that it cannot be maintained for much longer. At the beginning of his third term as Provost, in 1813, he resolves to abandon his past practice of governing 'with a sort of sinister respect for my own interests' (p. 259). Instead he will 'partake of the purer spirit which the great mutations of the age had conjured into public affairs' (p. 259).

He tells us that in the immediate past, 'Men in power then ruled more for their own ends than in these latter times; and use and wont sanctioned and sanctified many doings, from the days of our ancestors, that, but to imagine, will astonish and startle posterity' (p. 262). He is unblushing about these practices but has recognised that the old ways cannot continue. Still, having profited from the old, he can embrace the new with equanimity.

The way that a politician can conflate public good with private profit is a theme which recurs throughout the novel (and which is not unknown in the present day). Every scheme of Pawkie's which is intended to bring him a benefit is justified as being merely a by-product of a greater public good. There are examples given in Chapter 15 when the streets were improved with Pawkie boasting that he had instituted competitive tendering for the first time but admitting that both he and Bailie McLucre had personally benefitted, and in Chapter 20 when Pawkie gets the contract to supply the uniforms of the volunteers and gives himself 'my share of the advantage which the kingdom at large drew, in that period of anarchy and confusion, from the laudable establishment of a volunteer force' (p. 221).

There is no limit to the way in which Pawkie, and by implication real politicians, can rationalise illegitimate actions. When Pawkie is considering a plan by which he can more easily rule the council he is not deterred by legal constraints:

> I will no equivocate that there was, in this notion, an appearance of taking more on me than the laws allowed; but then my motives were so clean to my conscience, and I was so sure of satisfying the people by the methods I intended to pursue, that there could be no moral fault in the trifle of illegality, which, may be, I might have been led on to commit. (p. 263)

This raises interesting questions about moral relativism. How far should the actions of a person be judged by absolute and immutable standards and how far by those commonly prevailing at the time those actions occurred? Pawkie bends to the prevailing breeze but it is also, of course, the case that Pawkie has, by this stage in his life, made a great deal of money and 'had less incitement to be so grippy' (p. 259). He can therefore afford to be more careful with the public money and to be stricter in observing the proprieties.

Dealing with Democracy
The democratising ideals of the French Revolution were, in the early stages, welcomed by many in Britain who hoped that it might spur reform of government in this country. As the Terror developed and the Napoleonic wars began that welcome

was replaced, certainly on the part of the authorities and men of property, by a surge of patriotism and a fear of democratic infection. Galt takes a typically sideways look at these events.

He gives an account of the arrest of a French spy who turns out to be an innocent pastrycook (p. 206) and uses it to show how mass hysteria and mob justice can override common sense. He then goes on to show how the patriotic impulse can be overlaid by selfish concerns. The Burgh of Irvine voted in 1793 to give a bounty of ten guineas to each man who volunteered in Colonel Montgomerie's regiment of fencibles 'which is currently being raised'. Galt uses the raising of the volunteers to demonstrate that rank and power are as significant motivations as patriotism for some men (p. 219) while profit, as always with Pawkie who will supply the uniforms, is uppermost for others (p. 221).

Galt also seems to regard the paranoia of the Establishment as misplaced. When Pawkie learns about the proposal for a newspaper to be published by a reform-minded lawyer and 'three or four young and inexperienced lads that were wont to read essays' (p. 252), he is concerned that the newspaper would not be altogether clean of the 'coom [dirt] of jacobinical democracy' (p. 252). Pawkie's response is not to attempt to prosecute or harass the newspaper but to assimilate the lawyer into the elite of the town, flatter him and let the politics wither away.

In Irvine the council was less relaxed. On 17 April 1801 one of the bailies received a letter informing him that there was a plot to 'murder and burn all the most respectable men in this place'. On 27 April the council wrote to the commander of HM Forces in Scotland requesting a company of Foot to deal with the threat, and then on 22 May there is a call to the sheriff at Ayr to issue a warrant for the arrest of John Allen and William Muir for sedition, although the evidence adduced appears to be very flimsy.

Pawkie is an opportunist who considers new ideas from the point of view of how they might either provide scope for his advancement in wealth or power or threaten it. He is no democrat nor is he a deep thinker but he is far too shrewd to resist change on principle, not that principles ever detain him for very long. He can reconcile himself to whatever new dispensations seem likely to prevail. Thus he foresees the coming of political reform as 'the purer spirit which the great mutations of the age had conjured into public affairs' and therefore he needs to modify his behaviour before he becomes a victim of that change (p. 259).

Nevertheless, he has not lost his old cunning. When he is approaching retirement he thinks that the council ought to recognise his long and meritorious service but sees no sign that it will do so yet considers that 'something was of right due to me' (p. 267). And 'seeing that nothing was moving onwards in men's minds to do the act of courtesy to me, so justly my due', he wants to make certain that it happens (p. 268). He therefore sets out in some detail how he manipulates an inexperienced councillor to ensure that he is eventually given 'a very handsome silver cup, bearing an inscription in the Latin tongue' (p. 269).

Gender
As with all their traits, Galt takes a nuanced approach to his principal characters' relations with the opposite sex. Provost Pawkie is certainly not a romantic. He determines to get married when he finds 'by my books that I was in a way to do so' (p. 187) and the lady he chooses is not described by reference to her beauty but to the prospect of an inheritance from her mother. There is never any mention of love but as the years go on there are unmistakable signs of satisfaction and contentment on both sides, as shown in the introduction where the now widowed Mrs Pawkie shows evidence of 'the veneration in which Mr Pawkie had been through life regarded by his helpmate' (p. 185).

Nor does Pawkie look for romanticism in others. The assistant minister, Mr Pittle, is said to be attracted to Mrs Pawkie's cousin Miss Lizy Pinkie 'on account of the legacy of seven hundred pounds left her by an uncle' (p. 197). In Pawkie's account neither of the couple is an attractive prospect. He is both boring and mean and she is getting older and turning to the bottle but what stirs Pawkie to action in the matter is the possibility that Miss Lizy might 'outlive her income and [as a near relative] in her old age become a cess [burden] upon us' (p. 197). He is therefore very much concerned to promote the match and get Miss Lizy off their hands.

Pawkie certainly does not interest himself in other women. After his marriage his only relationships with women arise from his shop or his council business, and these are few. Outside his home he moves in a very male world. Women could not become councillors, and although they might own businesses they were not expected to play any prominent role in the town's affairs. Male and female lives tended to be very separate. The birth of Mrs Pawkie's second child must have been a difficult one: Mr Pawkie tells us that 'she had what was called a sore time o't' (p. 188). It is that 'what was called' which is instructive. He cannot simply say 'she had a hard time' but has to distance himself from any pronouncement on or knowledge of 'women's matters' by telling us that others had expressed that opinion.

Religion
Pawkie only takes an interest in religion when it provides a means for him to secure an advantage. As in Dalmailing the heritors of the parish were responsible for the appointment of the parish minister and for his stipend, manse and sundry other tasks such as poor relief and education. The difference was that in Irvine, being a royal burgh, three quarters of that responsibility rested with the council and the remainder with

the 'other heritors'. It is this that gives Pawkie the opportunity to have a major influence in the appointment of Mr Pittle. It also allows him, as can be seen in Chapter 16, to become involved when there is a need for repairs to the kirk in Gudetown. Galt uses that to show Provost Pawkie typically scheming to rent out the pews to raise the money for the repairs, thus saving a demand on the heritors.

This was again based on fact. The Reverend James Richmond, the minister of Irvine, records in the *Statistical Account* that for the heritors 'the money raised in this manner [pew rents] defrayed their share of the expense of building the church, and left them an overplus of near £300'.

The only other time when Pawkie becomes involved with religion is when Mr Pittle dies and the council has to choose his successor. He adopts a pious mien and religiose language to 'get a shepherd that would gather back to the establishment the flock which had been scattered among the seceders' (p. 262). Even that has unintended consequences since the chosen minister requires a better stipend, which drives the council to devise money-making schemes such as building a toll bridge. Galt is showing here how the trail of causation in public affairs is anything but straightforward.

Class

The *Statistical Account* provides some surprising facts about the composition of the labour force for a town of 4,500 people. It shows for Irvine that there were 116 weavers, fifty-six shoemakers, eighty masons and wrights, twenty-seven tailors and 150 colliers. There were seventy girls employed in tambour work. In a separate category was the very small number of professionals. There was one doctor and five lawyers, which suggests that the population tended to look after their own health but required qualified help for their business and property affairs.

At the bottom of the social heap were the feckless and indigent, among whom, as today, were poor souls who suffered from mental problems, as exemplified by Jennie Gaffaw and her daughter Meg in Chapters 24 and 38 of the *Annals,* or women who conceived out of wedlock, as Jean Gaisling in Chapter 9 of *The Provost*. Producing bastards or being proved guilty of the sin of fornication put women outside the pale of respectability although, unsurprisingly, the men involved, while they might have to suffer the cutty stool, as Burns did, were not so ostracised.

One of Galt's concerns is to show that the boundaries between the classes were becoming more porous and the relationships were changing. Pawkie's growing wealth enables his daughters to grow 'into young ladies' which entitled them 'to hold their heads something above the trades' (p. 239). The implication is that, as a small shopkeeper when he started out, he has now become a considerable merchant and thus, together with his standing as a Provost, is elevated to a higher social plane.

More significant, perhaps, is the changing relationship between the urban and rural elites. Pawkie recalls in Chapter 34 that traders such as himself 'came in for our share of the condescensions of the country gentry' (p. 244) but he notes that 'there was a gradual mixing in of the country gentry among the town's folks' (p. 243). The reason is ascribed partly to the French Revolution which caused 'men of substance to relax their ancient maxims of family pride and consequence' (p. 243) and partly to 'the great increase and growth of wealth which the influx of trade caused throughout the kingdom whereby the merchants were enabled to vie and ostentate even with the better sort of lairds' (p. 243). Thus the tables are turned, and:

> We discovered that they were vessels made of ordinary human clay; so that, instead of our reverence for them being

augmented by a freer intercourse, we thought less and less of them, until, poor bodies, the bit prideful lairdies were just looked down upon by our gauzie big-bellied burgesses, not a few of whom had heritable bonds on their estates. (p. 244)

The above passage relates to the merchants looking upwards but Pawkie also looks in the other direction. He 'never indeed could well understand how it would advantage, either the king or his ministers, to injure and do detriment to the lieges', instead believing that they 'should have a great interest in the prosperity and well-doing of the people' (p. 252). He also says that, 'I have had occasion to observe in the course of my experience that there is not a greater mollifier of the temper and nature of man than a constant flowing in of success and prosperity' (p. 210). Galt is therefore not afraid of class mobility. If the burgesses can get on to an equal footing with the landed interests so can the working classes rise if they have the education and the enterprise.

In both novels it is the weavers who are shown to be in the forefront of the adoption of radical ideas. Pawkie, in his inimitable way, accounts for this by saying that weavers and shoemakers are 'sedentary orders' who 'by the nature of sitting long in one posture, are apt to become subject to the flatulence of theoretical opinions' (p. 216).

Like Micah Balwhidder, James Pawkie recognised the effects of increased prosperity and the advent of innovations and new infrastructure. He makes a reference to the advantage which James Watt has brought 'to the ettling [aspiring] town of Greenock' by improving steam engines (p. 241). He also shows the many improvements which are made to the town in the way of paving the streets, provision of lamps, new bridges and public buildings, indicating a rising prosperity as a result of new industry and enterprise. Nevertheless, he knows that nothing comes for free and reflects that 'almost the whole tot

John Galt's *Annals of the Parish* and *The Provost*   59

of our improvements became, in a manner, the parents of new plagues' (p. 250).

Language
James Pawkie has sufficient education to read, write and count but his rise in the world in both business and politics is based on native shrewdness allied to powers of observation. Any direct speech in this novel is recounted to us by Mr Pawkie and it sounds so natural that the reader tends to forget that it must have been recollected by Pawkie, often from a long time ago. Given what we learn about Pawkie's propensity for self-justification and what Coleridge called 'his happy state of constant self-applause', we may be entitled to wonder how accurate his memory is. The language is, however, accurate and, like the *Annals*, dialogue sounds natural but is not verbatim. A look at any transcript of a real conversation will reveal hesitancies, repetitions and stock phrases used to buy thinking time. If truly accurate speech was reproduced in a novel the reader would lose interest. The skill, which Galt had, is to make the speech sound like real talk while advancing the novel without losing the reader's attention.

Pawkie has sufficient education to be a successful businessman but he is not a learned man. His innate cunning means that he tailors the breadth of his speech to his interlocutor and to the purposes he is trying to achieve. He therefore uses a variety of different registers. He uses Scots for local incidents but English when he wishes to be formal or to impress his readers. As Derrick McClure puts it, Pawkie 'prefers English as a language of moralising and reflection'. McClure goes further by saying that 'Galt's use of language contributes in large measure to [...] the self-revelation of the narrators'. Pawkie uses broad Scots when trying to win other councillors to his side of the argument. Even when he does not use Scots words he is clearly speaking in a Scots accent. When he addresses Mr Smeddum with 'It's very extraordinar [...] that nobody has seen a' this but yoursel'' (p. 215) then the use of 'extraordinar', 'a'' and 'yoursel' indicate that he is using the conventional speech of Irvine to one of his social equals. Pawkie knows, as Graham Tulloch notes, 'that he is at his most persuasive when playing the role of the plain man'.

When he wishes not so much to be persuasive but to carry his point against a weaker opponent he uses the weight and formality of English. Thus he browbeats Mr Pittle into marrying his relative with a five-line speech in which only the final word, 'poopit' [pulpit] is Scots (p. 199). To his superiors he also uses English although on these occasions it is to demonstrate his education and suitability for office. His proposal to the Earl that he should act as his lordship's proxy is couched entirely in English of a formal kind (p. 206).

The Provost, like the *Annals,* is written in a plain style as is consistent with a man of Pawkie's education and upbringing. The exception is the introduction, where Galt satirises himself. He hints that he is the author of the *Annals* and then launches into a high-flown, unnecessarily verbose report of his dealings with Pawkie's widow which is completely at odds with the text which follows. The ornate language does not completely hide practical issues. He persuades the widow to let him edit the supposed autobiography by 'an indirect proposal to share the profits' (p. 285).

Nominative Determinism

Galt evolved a system for naming the people in his books. In the *Annals* most of the principal characters have unremarkable names. Balwhidder, Malcolm, and Macadam are ordinary surnames as are those of his first and third wives, Lanshaw and Nugent, but Balwhidder's second wife, who grew up on a farm famous for cheese, is called Kibbock; 'kebbock' is the Scots word for a whole cheese. It is significant that the first and third Mrs Balwhidders are little more than ciphers while the second plays a starring role. Then there is Mr Cayenne, who has made a fortune in the Americas and is a distinctly peppery character. We therefore see that Galt uses character or trade in finding names for his creations.

With some of the incidental characters we begin to see the pattern. In the *Annals* the gamekeeper is Nichol Snipe and the mentally disabled woman is Jenny Gaffaw. This pattern becomes much more pronounced in *The Provost*, beginning with the name of the protagonist, James Pawkie. 'Pawkie' is defined in the *Concise Scots Dictionary* as 'wily, crafty' and 'as having a humorously critical outlook on life, characterised by a sly, quiet wit'. This is Provost Pawkie to the life.

The Provost's chief rival on the council is Bailie McLucre, who is, according to Pawkie, obsessed with money (although no more so than Pawkie himself). The argumentative tobacconist is Mr Smeddum, which not only denotes spirit and energy but is also a fine powder, like snuff. Tradesmen tend to be named after their calling, as in Mr Pipe the wine merchant, Mr Plane the joiner, Mr Girdwood the cooper and Dr Whackdeil the minister. Even in this system Galt finds the opportunity to slip in a sly joke. Dialect words, used for ironic effect, recur constantly in the names he gives his characters, especially those which relate to their professions. In *The Provost* the two schoolmasters are Mr Dinledoup ('Hitbottom') and Mr Scudmyloof ('Smackpalm') (p. 255). Even here, with these minor characters, Galt draws a subtle distinction. Mr Dinledoup is the older, sterner and more traditional dominie: Mr Scudmyloof is the younger, more progressive and therefore relatively less harsh teacher.

Self-revelation
Pawkie often employs deliberate dissimulation to gain his ends. That does not, of course, prevent him from rationalising his behaviour in a way which justifies it to his own conscience. The reader has to interpret that behaviour for her or himself and draw their own conclusions. Some readers, and there are

examples given below in the quoted reviews, saw Pawkie as no more than a loveable rogue with a principally comic function. They did not see, or chose to ignore, the all-pervasive corruption of which he was such a master. This is the danger of irony: that the hidden meaning may not be discerned.

The dissimulation, at least to himself if not to the reader, is perhaps exemplified best throughout Chapter 10 where Pawkie describes a commotion on the occasion of the king's birthday. The council decides not to gift the traditional cart of coals to the townsfolk for a bonfire but does continue the practice of providing for the councillors to drink a bowl of punch at the cross. A dispassionate reading of the event shows that Pawkie is stubborn and arrogant, over-reacts to the situation and misreads the temper of the mob. Yet he presents himself as cool and steadfast. It is Major Target who saves the day but Pawkie has to claim the credit for himself because he sent to Ayr for a detachment of soldiers who could not arrive until long after the townsfolk had dispersed.

The long-term effect is that ever since that day soldiers were quartered in Gudetown, which Pawkie does not like; but rather than see that as the consequence of his own hasty actions he ascribes it to 'rebellion and treasonable practices' (p. 204). There are similar examples throughout the book where Pawkie is boasting of his cleverness while the reader is receiving an entirely different message.

It is significant too that Pawkie's private thoughts, as set down in his autobiography, are at odds with the persona he tries to project in public. The man who has said that he wanted to 'rule without being felt' and that it was better to have than to show power and influence is himself shown in his own mind as revelling in the possession and exercise of both. Galt is showing us the gap which can exist between private and public personas, especially among those who are in positions of authority. He is reminding us that it is human nature to present ourselves in the best possible light but that others may interpret our actions and words in a very different way from that which we intend.

Reception and Criticism
In the reviews *The Provost* tended to suffer by comparison with the *Annals*. *The Literary Chronicle and Weekly Review* of June 22 1823 says that it is a companion and that 'no library which possesses the one can be complete without the other', and while *The Provost* is good 'the author [...] might have made it much better'. *The Literary Gazette* of the same date felt that it fell 'well short of the standard' of the *Annals*. It went on to offer the opinion that Galt's works 'display very peculiar powers for painting national manners in certain classes, and are exceedingly unequal, not to say inferior whenever they are exercised out of that boundary'.

The Ladies' Monthly Museum of July 1822 agrees that it is an essential companion to *The Annals* but 'will not be held in equal estimation'. Incidentally, it is worth quoting this publication's masthead in full as an example of attitudes to women at that time. It is *The Ladies' Monthly Museum; or, polite repository of amusement and instruction; being an assemblage of whatever can tend to please the fancy, interest the mind, or exalt the character of the British fair*. It claims to be edited and published by 'A Society of Ladies'.

It is also indicative of how ingrained corruption was at that time that *The Edinburgh Review* of October 1823 comments on Pawkie's 'love of jobbing or little management, which is inseparable from the situation of a magistrate in one of our little Burghs' but concludes that 'his ends are not on the whole unjust or dishonest'.

Nevertheless, Galt's novels remained popular throughout the nineteenth century with publications and reprints by various publishers. An 1895 edition has an introduction by the hugely popular sentimental novelist S. R. Crockett. At the turn of the nineteenth and twentieth centuries Galt was erroneously stigmatised as a precursor of the Kailyard school of sentimental novels of Scottish rural life. Critics then were still blind to the truth of Galt's observations. Crockett suggests that 'the world would not be so very badly governed if all our rulers and magistrates were no worse than the excellent Provost of Gudetown'.

In more modern times, criticism of the novels has tended to be more balanced and to be more acute, finding depths which eluded the contemporary reviewers. That does not preclude idiosyncratic conclusions. Jennie Aberdein's biography *John Galt* (1936) sees Provost Pawkie not as a schemer intent on his own financial and political advancement but as a harmless comedy character, a loveable rogue who 'is never guilty of acting for self-interest to the detriment of the public good and we are amused at his conscientious distinctions'. Modern readers may draw different conclusions.

More modern scholars have tended to look beneath the surface of these novels. The economic historian Christopher Whatley says that 'Galt was one of Scotland's finest social commentators' and Keith Costain captures Galt's ambivalence about 'progress' in saying that 'Galt did not always believe that Adam Smith's "invisible hand" would somehow transform private vices into public benefits'. Katie Trumpener sums all this up by describing the relation between human agency and historical change in *The Provost* as:

> Once they have set in motion the new social apparatus, it not only maintains and perpetuates itself, constantly justifying the expansion of its own scope and operations, but also renders increasingly invisible the human agency that put it in place [...] Galt's novel masterfully presents both the human agency by which social change is effected (demonstrating clearly whose interests are served and whose repressed) and how the machinery of change, once put into operation,

camouflages this agency as the movement of history, freeing the manipulators to appear, even to themselves, as public benefactors.

It is debatable whether Galt himself would have analysed his work in that way but it is a testament to his powers of observation and fidelity to the truth of what he observed that these texts allow modern critics to trace the effects of the changes he documented in the light of two hundred years of subsequent history.

Evaluating both novels, Ian Gordon says that 'the quiet art of the *Annals* has a quite deceptive simplicity', but he has stronger praise for *The Provost* which is 'a brilliant fusion [...] of the small-town Scottish scene and the world of political action'. He notes that Galt had long been fascinated by Machiavelli and, from his work in and around parliament, the exercise of political power. He goes on to say that *The Provost* is, as we have seen, 'comedy with serious overtones not recognised by his early readers'.

6. CONCLUSION

There are many good reasons for reading *Annals of the Parish* and *The Provost* today. They can be seen as portraits of a Scotland which was in the throes of changing from a largely agrarian society to one which had to cope with new technology and concomitant social change; they can be mined for social and historical evidence and atmosphere; or simply as a series of more or less humorous episodes recounted by fallible but recognisably human characters. These categories are not mutually exclusive.

Galt recognised that comedy, often unintentional, was a prime characteristic of human behaviour and used it liberally to illuminate both its good and bad aspects. Sometimes, as can be seen in the reception of the novels, his intentions were misconstrued. The perceptive reader will, however, take satisfaction from the way the various aspects of these novels are woven together so that art is used in the service of truth.

7. FURTHER READING

Primary Texts

John Galt, *Annals of the Parish*, in *Four Galt Novels*, Ian Campbell (ed.), Edinburgh, Kennedy & Boyd, 2015

John Galt, *The Provost*, in *Four Galt Novels*, Ian Campbell (ed.), Edinburgh, Kennedy & Boyd, 2015

Secondary Texts

John Galt, *The Autobiography,* London, Cochrane & McCrone, 1833

John Galt, *My Literary Life and Miscellanies,* Edinburgh, William Blackwood, 1834

John Galt, Introduction to *The Seamstress,* in *Selected Short Stories,* Ian A. Gordon (ed.), Edinburgh, Scottish Academic Press, 1978

Jennie W. Aberdein, *John Galt*, London, Oxford University Press, 1936

Gerard Carruthers and Colin Kidd (eds), *The International Companion to John Galt*, Glasgow, Scottish Literature International, 2017

Keith Costain, 'The Prince and the Provost', in *Studies in Scottish Literature* 6, July 1968–April 1969, Columbia, University of Carolina Press, 1969

T. M. Devine, *The Scottish Nation 1700–2000,* London, Penguin, 1999

Duncan Forbes, *Adam Ferguson and the Idea of Community,* in *Edinburgh in the Age of Reason,* Edinburgh, Edinburgh University Press, 1967

Ian A. Gordon, *John Galt: The Life of a Writer,* Toronto, Toronto University Press, 1972

Ian A. Gordon, Introduction to John Galt, *The Provost,* Oxford, Oxford University Press, 1982

Regina Hewitt (ed.), *John Galt: Observations and Conjectures on Literature, History, and Society*, Lewisburg, Bucknell University Press, 2012

Robert C. Lee, *The Canada Company and the Huron Tract*, Toronto, Natural Heritage Books, 2004

Ursula K. Le Guin, 'B-Sides: John Galt's *Annals of the Parish*', in *Public Books*, at **www.publicbooks.org/b-sides-john-galts-annals-parish**

Emma Letley, *From Galt to Douglas Brown*, Edinburgh, Scottish Academic Press, 1988

Arthur Lower, *A History of Canada*, Don Mills, Longmans, 1964

Frank H. Lyell, *A Study of the Novels of John Galt*, Princeton, Princeton University Press, 1942

Michael Lynch, *Scotland: A New History*, London, Pimlico, 1991

J. Derrick McClure, 'Scots and English in *Annals of the Parish* and *The Provost*', in *John Galt 1779–1979*, C. A. Whatley (ed.), Edinburgh, Ramsay Head Press, 1979

Kenneth McNeil, 'Time, Emigration, and the Circum-Atlantic World: John Galt's "Bogle Corbet"', in *John Galt: Observations and Conjectures on Literature, History, and Society,* Regina Hewitt (ed.), Lewisburg, Bucknell University Press, 2012

Paul Scott, *John Galt,* Edinburgh, Scottish Academic Press, 1985

Kenneth Simpson, *The Protean Scot*, Aberdeen, Aberdeen University Press, 1988

Dugald Stewart, 'Theoretical or Conjectural History' in *The Scottish Enlightenment: An Anthology*, Alexander Broadie (ed.), Edinburgh, Canongate Press, 1997

H. B. Timothy, *The Galts: A Canadian Odyssey*, Toronto, McLelland & Stewart, 1977

Katie Trumpener, *Bardic Nationalism*, Princeton, Princeton University Press, 1997

Graham Tulloch, 'The Use of Scots in Scott and other nineteenth century novelists', in *Scott and His Influence: The Papers of the Aberdeen Scott Conference 1982,* J. H. Alexander and D. Hewitt (eds), Aberdeen, ASLS, 1983

Christopher Whatley (ed.), '*Annals of the Parish* and History', in *John Galt 1779–1979,* Edinburgh, Ramsay Head Press, 1979

Nicholas Whistler, *John Galt and the New World,* Cambridge University PhD thesis, 1992

Lightning Source UK Ltd.
Milton Keynes UK
UKHW02f2352110518
322483UK00005B/253/P